AF316832

DAILY CHRISTIAN AFFIRMATIONS *FOR* TEEN GIRLS

365 Encouraging Bible Verses for Young Women

MADE EASY PRESS

Producer & International Distributor
eBookPro Publishing
www.ebook-pro.com

DAILY CHRISTIAN AFFIRMATIONS FOR TEEN GIRLS
Encouraging Bible Verses for Young Women
Made Easy Press

Contact: agency@ebook-pro.com

ISBN 9789655753684

This book belongs to

....

Introduction

Navigating the world as a teenage girl is a challenge. There's a lot to deal with, like school, extracurricular activities, chores, friends, romantic relationships, and physical changes, all while growing up and figuring yourself out as a person.

It can be overwhelming, and you might sometimes feel that it's all too much.

But God's Word can help you get through anything – even the challenging teenage years.

This little book is a well of encouragement, inspiration, and wisdom, to boost your confidence through a whole year.

Every day for 52 weeks, Monday through Sunday, you will find an empowering affirmation reminding you just how strong, brave, capable, and beautiful you are, and of all the wonderful things God has in store for you!

And the best thing is – you can start right away, next Monday!

Keep this book by your bed or on your desk, somewhere close at hand, and clear two minutes each morning to start the day with a confidence-boosting, thought-provoking dose of self-love.

Day **1:**

Monday

I will take the time to appreciate
quiet moments this morning.

Day **2:**

Tuesday

I follow Jesus no matter
where he leads me.

Day **3:**

Wednesday

I am beautiful by God's definition.

Day **4:**

Thursday

I can do anything I put my mind to.

Friday

I am creatively inspired
by the world around me.

Saturday

I have the power to thrive.

Sunday

Positivity is a choice
that I choose to make.

Day 8:

Monday

I am excited to take in new experiences
and gain knowledge.

Day 9:

Tuesday

I can handle anything life throws at me.

Day 10:

Wednesday

I am confident in the presence of others.

Day 11:

Thursday

I love all of God's creatures,
including people, animals, and plants.

Day 12:

Friday

When I feel overwhelmed,
I cry out to God and find safety.

Day 13:

Saturday

I put God first in my life.

Day 14:

Sunday

God has exceptional things
in store for me.

Day **15:**

Monday

I will find God when I seek him
with all of my heart.

Day **16:**

Tuesday

I am a role model to my siblings,
cousins, and friends.

Day **17:**

Wednesday

My hard work will pay off.

Day **18:**

Thursday

I don't need anyone else
to tell me I am worthy.

Friday

I am a good person who deserves
happiness, health, and peace.

Day **20**:

Saturday

I am capable of making positive choices
that lead me to what I want.

Day **21**:

Sunday

I have friends who love me.

Day **22:**

Monday

I guard my heart because it
determines the course of my life.

Day **23:**

Tuesday

Nothing can stop me
from achieving my dreams.

Day **24:**

Wednesday

There is so much for me
to see and experience.

Day **25:**

Thursday

I am in harmony and balance with life.

Friday

I am wonderfully made.

Saturday

Success is within my reach.

Sunday

I am in charge of how I feel
and I choose to feel happy.

Day **29:**

Monday

I have my own sense of style
and it is unique.

Day **30:**

Tuesday

I have the peace of Christ.

Day **31:**

Wednesday

I focus on the positive things in my life.

Day **32:**

Thursday

No one else in the world is like me.

Day **33:**

Friday

I am grateful for everything that I have.

Day **34:**

Saturday

I am creative.

Day **35:**

Sunday

It's okay to be sad sometimes.

Day **36:**

Monday

I am faithful.

Day **37:**

Tuesday

I get to decide what is best for me.

Day **38:**

Wednesday

There are people I haven't met yet
who will become an important part of my life.

Day **39:**

Thursday

I live with kindness.

Friday

I persevere.

Day 41:

Saturday

I am loved just as I am.

Day 42:

Sunday

Other people's words
cannot hurt me.

17

Day **43:**

Monday

My prayers will be answered by God.

Day **44:**

Tuesday

I can find joy even in the smallest things.

Day **45:**

Wednesday

I can rely on God.

Day **46:**

Thursday

I am becoming closer to
my true self every day.

Friday

I can have wisdom and guidance
from God if I just ask.

Saturday

I am peaceful and whole.

Sunday

I take the time to appreciate
the beautiful things I see.

Day 50:

Monday

I am created in God's image.

Day 51:

Tuesday

I appreciate all the gifts I have received.

Day 52:

Wednesday

My flaws are a part of me
and I embrace them.

Day 53:

Thursday

I am fortunate.

Day **54:**
Friday

I am beautiful, smart and talented.

Day **55:**
Saturday

God is my strength and shield.

Day **56:**
Sunday

God gives me strength.

Day **57:**

Monday

God loves those who love him.

Day **58:**

Tuesday

I have sound knowledge and wisdom.

Day **59:**

Wednesday

I am happy where I am in my life
right now.

Day **60:**

Thursday

I appreciate the body that God gave me.

Friday

I have the courage to do
challenging things.

Saturday

I am a unique gift to the world.

Sunday

I become a better version
of myself every day.

Day **64:**

Monday

I deflect negativity.

Day **65:**

Tuesday

I acknowledge that there is
a time and a place for everything.

Day **66:**

Wednesday

God chose me to be His.

Day **67:**

Thursday

I did the best that I could
at the moment.

Day 68:

Friday

I have everything I need to succeed.

Day 69:

Saturday

I am at peace with
who I am as a person.

Day 70:

Sunday

I am Jesus Christ's friend.

Day **71:**

Monday

As I place my hope in the Lord,
my strength is renewed.

Day **72:**

Tuesday

I enjoy helping others.

Day **73:**

Wednesday

I won't settle for less than I deserve.

Day **74:**

Thursday

I can do hard things.

Friday

God is looking after me.

Saturday

I don't have to spend time
with people who make me feel bad.

Sunday

God is with me.

Week **12**

Day **78:**

Monday

I channel my anger into healthy outlets.

Day **79:**

Tuesday

I look for the good in each day.

Day **80:**

Wednesday

I am bold in my actions.

Day **81:**

Thursday

God is my refuge.

Friday

I let go of all negative emotions and fear.

Saturday

I have meaningful and equal relationships
with my friends and family.

Sunday

My trust lies in God alone.

Day 85:

Monday

The more I like myself,
the more others will like me.

Day 86:

Tuesday

My life is filled with beauty and grace.

Day 87:

Wednesday

I am surrounded by positive
and supportive people.

Day 88:

Thursday

I strive for improvement,
not for perfection.

Day **89**:

Friday

God guides me with love.

Day **90**:

Saturday

I can show my devotion to God
by loving everyone.

Day **91**:

Sunday

I respect my body for the
unique way it is made.

Day **92:**

Monday

I am beautiful both inside and out.

Day **93:**

Tuesday

In ten years, I will be exactly
where I want to be.

Day **94:**

Wednesday

I forgive myself for past mistakes.

Day **95:**

Thursday

I am open to limitless possibilities.

Day 96:

Friday

How other people talk or act
doesn't reflect on me.

Day 97:

Saturday

I am grateful for all that
God has given me.

Day 98:

Sunday

I may be young, but that doesn't
mean I don't have worth.

Week **15**

Day **99**:

Monday

My mistakes don't define me.

Day **100**:

Tuesday

My voice matters.

Day **101**:

Wednesday

Challenges are what make my life interesting.

Day **102**:

Thursday

I have countless skills and talents.

Day **103:**

Friday

I don't need to follow along
with what everyone else is doing.

Day **104:**

Saturday

I have might and power.

Day **105:**

Sunday

I am smart.

Week **16**

Day 106:

Monday

I belong where I am.

Day 107:

Tuesday

I am kind to people and animals.

Day 108:

Wednesday

There is no one else in the world
who is exactly like me.

Day 109:

Thursday

I am blessed.

Friday

I make time to care for myself.

Saturday

I am sensitive and human.

Sunday

I am a light that
shines on the world.

Day 113:

Monday

I am allowed to ask for
what I want and what I need.

Day 114:

Tuesday

I have all that I need.

Day 115:

Wednesday

I rise above gossip and
talking rudely about others.

Day 116:

Thursday

My body is beautiful just the way it is.

Day **117:**

Friday

Each day is a blessing and a gift.

Day **118:**

Saturday

I honor my parents
and do what they ask of me.

Day **119:**

Sunday

There is nothing too hard for God.

Week **18**

Day **120:**

Monday

It is enough to do my best.

Day **121:**

Tuesday

I am patient.

Day **122:**

Wednesday

Today is going to be a really,
really great day.

Day **123:**

Thursday

I learn from each relationship,
even if it doesn't work out.

Day 124:

Friday

No one in the world is perfect.

Day 125:

Saturday

I make good choices.

Day 126:

Sunday

God knows my deepest
thoughts and hopes.

Day **127:**

Monday

God will supply all my needs.

Day **128:**

Tuesday

I am not afraid to work hard.

Day **129:**

Wednesday

It's okay that I have different
interests than my friends.

Day **130:**

Thursday

I am on an adventure
to discover myself.

Day **131:**

Friday

I speak with love.

Day **132:**

Saturday

God fights for me.

Day **133:**

Sunday

God woke me up this morning
for a purpose.

Day **134:**

Monday

I have hobbies and interests of my own.

Day **135:**

Tuesday

I am responsible for myself.

Day **136:**

Wednesday

Life does not have to be perfect
to be wonderful.

Day **137:**

Thursday

I have confidence in God's power.

Day 138:

Friday

I have goals and dreams
that I am going to achieve.

Day 139:

Saturday

My head is full of new ideas.

Day 140:

Sunday

I choose hope.

Day **141:**

Monday

It's okay for me to have fun.

Day **142:**

Tuesday

My roots teach me who I am.

Day **143:**

Wednesday

I am enough.

Day **144:**

Thursday

I am God's beloved daughter.

Day **145:**

Friday

Everything about me is intentionally
designed by God.

Day **146:**

Saturday

I can choose to do things
differently from others.

Day **147:**

Sunday

I love who I am right now.

Day **148**:

Monday

God's Spirit makes me feel powerful.

Day **149**:

Tuesday

I am learning to love myself
the way God does.

Day **150**:

Wednesday

I will not worry about the future.

Day **151**:

Thursday

I appreciate myself for all I do.

Friday

God's power works best
in my weakness.

Saturday

I appreciate the life that God gave me.

Sunday

Wonderful things are going
to happen to me.

Day 155:

Monday

I am open and honest with my feelings.

Day 156:

Tuesday

I appreciate every creation of God.

Day 157:

Wednesday

"Normal" isn't real.
I am unique and that is beautiful.

Day 158:

Thursday

It's okay to admit when I am wrong
and to ask for forgiveness.

Friday

God does not forsake
those who seek Him.

Saturday

I care about the environment.

Sunday

I am healthy.

Week **24**

Day 162:

Monday

I can forgive myself.

Day 163:

Tuesday

My faith makes me whole.

Day 164:

Wednesday

I am a good and caring friend.

Day 165:

Thursday

I have a community that cares about me.

Friday

Language is powerful.
I choose the words I say carefully.

Day **167**:

Saturday

I am open to receiving advice
from people with more wisdom than me.

Day **168**:

Sunday

I am keeping my body
safe and healthy.

Day **169:**

Monday

I am happy to be alive.

Day **170:**

Tuesday

I am safe in God's care.

Day **171:**

Wednesday

My feelings deserve recognition.

Day **172:**

Thursday

I am a good, law-abiding citizen.

Day **173**:

Friday

I am a woman of discipline
and self-control.

Day **174**:

Saturday

I stand up for myself
because I matter.

Day **175**:

Sunday

I trust myself to make
the right decision.

Day **176:**

Monday

I am loved by God.

Day **177:**

Tuesday

I am part of God's huge family.

Day **178:**

Wednesday

I don't have to be the center of attention.

Day **179:**

Thursday

I can change the world.

Day 180:

Friday

I am whole and complete.

Day 181:

Saturday

God is always with me.

Day 182:

Sunday

I am content.

Day 183:

Monday

I can talk to God about anything.

Day 184:

Tuesday

My first love will probably not be
my only love, and that's okay.

Day 185:

Wednesday

I live in the moment.

Day 186:

Thursday

There will always be bumps in the road.

Day **187**:

Friday

I am my own best friend.

Day **188**:

Saturday

God listens to me.

Day **189**:

Sunday

God will give me the strength I need to do everything He wants me to do today.

Week **28**

Day **190:**

Monday

I am in control of my thoughts.

Day **191:**

Tuesday

I am beautiful.

Day **192:**

Wednesday

Simple things can make me happy.

Day **193:**

Thursday

I am important to so many people.

Day 194:

Friday

I will do great things.

Day 195:

Saturday

I accept myself for who I am.

Day 196:

Sunday

I am not too much for God to handle.

Day 197:

Monday

My trust is in the Lord.

Day 198:

Tuesday

There's always something
new for me to learn.

Day 199:

Wednesday

I am doing a great job growing up.

Day 200:

Thursday

I make choices that honor my body.

Friday

If I ever struggle, I have people
who will help me.

Day **202**:

Saturday

God will never leave or forsake me.

Day **203**:

Sunday

I live in the present.

Day **204:**

Monday

I keep my online posting
positive and affirming.

Day **205:**

Tuesday

I am capable of unconditional love.

Day **206:**

Wednesday

I can control how I respond
to things that bother me.

Day **207:**

Thursday

I have confidence that I can do
all things through Christ.

Friday

Challenges make me
stronger and wiser.

Day **209**:

Saturday

I am willing to ask for what I need.

Day **210**:

Sunday

I am responsible
with my technology.

Day 211:

Monday

I put my energy into things
that matter to me.

Day 212:

Tuesday

I know how to be still
so I can hear from God.

Day 213:

Wednesday

My prayers are heard.

Day 214:

Thursday

I am empowered to shut down
conversations I am uncomfortable with
or that may hurt other people.

Day 215:

Friday

I trust God wholeheartedly.

Day 216:

Saturday

I like the person I am becoming.

Day 217:

Sunday

I am absolutely unique.

Day **218**:

Monday

I don't owe all of my time to anyone.

Day **219**:

Tuesday

I am complete as I am.

Day **220**:

Wednesday

I let go of regret.

Day **221**:

Thursday

I am a worthy child of God.

Day 222:

Friday

I do what I can.

Day 223:

Saturday

My confidence grows when I step
outside my comfort zone.

Day 224:

Sunday

My heart is open to all of the wisdom
the world has to offer.

Week 33

Day **225:**

Monday

If I mess up today,
I can try again tomorrow.

Day **226:**

Tuesday

I am empowered to be
the best version of myself.

Day **227:**

Wednesday

God is my stronghold in times of trouble.

Day **228:**

Thursday

I look forward to tomorrow
and the opportunities that await me.

Day 229:

Friday

Today, I will do something
that scares me.

Day 230:

Saturday

I am boundlessly strong
as God is with me.

Day 231:

Sunday

I am capable of changing my mind
when presented with new information.

Day **232:**

Monday

I am a little weird but so is everyone.

Day **233:**

Tuesday

It's okay to make mistakes.

Day **234:**

Wednesday

More people care about me
than I even know.

Day **235:**

Thursday

I love and respect my family
for all they do for me.

Day 236:

Friday

Everything will work out for me.

Day 237:

Saturday

My mind is full of brilliant ideas

Day 238:

Sunday

I represent the values that matter
to me and my community.

Day **239**:

Monday

God wants me to be happy.

Day **240**:

Tuesday

I am a living, breathing miracle.

Day **241**:

Wednesday

The people who judge me are the people who are most afraid of being judged.

Day **242**:

Thursday

I am free from expectations and criticism.

Day 243:

Friday

I learn from the word of God.

Day 244:

Saturday

I have a bright future ahead of me.

Day 245:

Sunday

I am optimistic because
today is a new day.

Week 36

Day 246:

Monday

I deserve to be surrounded
by people I love.

Day 247:

Tuesday

I have a positive mindset.

Day 248:

Wednesday

I am enough.

Day 249:

Thursday

Good things await me.

Day **250:**

Friday

My mind is clear.

Day **251:**

Saturday

My body is my own.

Day **252:**

Sunday

I take things one day at a time.

Day **253:**

Monday

Every day is a fresh start.

Day **254:**

Tuesday

I can tell my own story.

Day **255:**

Wednesday

I am open to new ways
of improving myself.

Day **256:**

Thursday

I am grateful for each breath
God gives me.

Day **257:**

Friday

I am a work of art.

Day **258:**

Saturday

I take pride in my ability to make
worthwhile contributions to the world.

Day **259:**

Sunday

I live every day to the fullest.

Day **260**:

Monday

I am smart, but I don't know everything.

Day **261**:

Tuesday

I can be soft in my heart
and firm in my boundaries.

Day **262**:

Wednesday

Changing my mind is a strength,
not a weakness.

Day **263**:

Thursday

I will do better next time.

Day 264:

Friday

Today I focus on God
to fill me with peace of mind.

Day 265:

Saturday

I care about what is going on
in the world.

Day 266:

Sunday

God is right here with me,
holding my hand.

Day 267:

Monday

With faith I am able to move mountains.

Day 268:

Tuesday

I embrace change
and rise to new opportunities.

Day 269:

Wednesday

I am the hero of my own story.

Day 270:

Thursday

I don't have to please anyone
other than myself.

Day 271:

Friday

The people I see on Instagram
are not perfect.

Day 272:

Saturday

I will respect myself and others because
we are all made in the image of God.

Day 273:

Sunday

I am walking in the wisdom of God.

Week **40**

Day **274:**

Monday

Happiness is within my grasp.

Day **275:**

Tuesday

Saying "no" makes me stronger.

Day **276:**

Wednesday

I stand up for what I believe in.

Day **277:**

Thursday

I live by faith.

Day 278:

Friday

God has great plans for my life.

Day 279:

Saturday

To show love to God,
I show love to myself.

Day 280:

Sunday

In five years, it will not matter
what I wore today.

Day **281:**

Monday

I let go of grudges.

Day **282:**

Tuesday

The Lord hears me
and answers me when I call Him.

Day **283:**

Wednesday

I release the pressure to excel.

Day **284:**

Thursday

God loves me with everlasting love.

Day **285:**

Friday

I will acknowledge God
in all of my ways.

Day **286:**

Saturday

I choose Godly things.

Day **287:**

Sunday

I have a family that loves me.

Day **288**:

Monday

It's okay to be proud of myself
and my accomplishments.

Day **289**:

Tuesday

Today will be a day to remember.

Day **290**:

Wednesday

I have a constant source of truth
in God's word.

Day **291**:

Thursday

I believe in myself as God believes in me.

Day 292:

Friday

I am kind and respectful to the elderly.

Day 293:

Saturday

I do not have to compare myself
to anyone else.

Day 294:

Sunday

I am everything God says I am.

Day **295:**

Monday

I am valued and helpful.

Day **296:**

Tuesday

I am loved by God
more than I can imagine.

Day **297:**

Wednesday

I am held and supported
by those who love me.

Day **298:**

Thursday

I am accepted by God.

Day **299:**

Friday

Even my wildest dreams can come true.

Day **300:**

Saturday

God is looking out for me.

Day **301:**

Sunday

I don't need likes and comments
to be fulfilled.

Day **302:**

Monday

My future is mine to choose.

Day **303:**

Tuesday

Just because I haven't reached my destination
doesn't mean that I am lost.

Day **304:**

Wednesday

I deserve a loving and equal
romantic relationship.

Day **305:**

Thursday

I am learning valuable lessons
from myself every day.

Day 306:

Friday

I am saved.

Day 307:

Saturday

I have control over
my thoughts and words.

Day 308:

Sunday

I have the power
to face any difficulty.

Day **309:**

Monday

I am God's precious child.

Day **310:**

Tuesday

Fear has no place in my life.

Day **311:**

Wednesday

I am relaxed and happy with where I am.

Day **312:**

Thursday

I do not pretend to be anyone
or anything other than who I am.

Day **313:**

Friday

I don't have to participate
if I don't want to.

Day **314:**

Saturday

Growing up is an adventure.

Day **315:**

Sunday

God's faithfulness is new
every morning.

Day **316:**

Monday

I am focused on what matters most.

Day **317:**

Tuesday

I am true to myself.

Day **318:**

Wednesday

I am growing up at my own pace.

Day **319:**

Thursday

I am a loving being.

Day 320:

Friday

Trying new things
opens new opportunities.

Day 321:

Saturday

My light cannot be extinguished.

Day 322:

Sunday

I may not have all the answers,
and I am okay with that.

Day **323:**

Monday

My worth is defined by His grace.

Day **324:**

Tuesday

I love with my whole heart.

Day **325:**

Wednesday

I radiate confidence.

Day **326:**

Thursday

I deserve the healthiest version of myself.

Day 327:

Friday

I trust that I am on the right path.

Day 328:

Saturday

I do not need drugs or alcohol
to have fun.

Day 329:

Sunday

My opinions are unique and important.

Day **330:**

Monday

My life is not a race or a competition.

Day **331:**

Tuesday

I trust God at all times.

Day **332:**

Wednesday

All my problems have solutions.

Day **333:**

Thursday

My focus is sharp.

Day 334:

Friday

As God was with Moses,
He will also be with me.

Day 335:

Saturday

I deserve to be happy.

Day 336:

Sunday

Every storm will pass.

Day **337:**

Monday

I do not have to reveal my whole self
on social media.

Day **338:**

Tuesday

I am allowed to feel good.

Day **339:**

Wednesday

I understand that my actions become habits,
so I will try to do the right thing.

Day **340:**

Thursday

God wants me to live.

Day **341**:

Friday

I invite art, music, and beauty
into my life.

Day **342**:

Saturday

I will commit my way to God
and trust in Him.

Day **343**:

Sunday

I have big dreams.

Week **50**

Day **344:**
Monday

I am proud of who I am.

Day **345:**
Tuesday

I am lucky to have the
opportunities that I do.

Day **346:**
Wednesday

I celebrate the good qualities
in others and myself.

Day **347:**
Thursday

I am never alone.

Day **348:**

Friday

I uplift the people around me.

Day **349:**

Saturday

My life is a gift.

Day **350:**

Sunday

It's okay to be scared sometimes.

Day **351**:

Monday

I am willing to accept help when offered.

Day **352**:

Tuesday

I breathe in positivity and
exhale negative thinking.

Day **353**:

Wednesday

Right now, I am exactly
what God created me to be.

Day **354**:

Thursday

I am fearless.

Day 355:

Friday

God's approval of me is most important.

Day 356:

Saturday

My sorrows will be turned into joy.

Day 357:

Sunday

I deserve friends that treat me
with equal love and kindness.

Day **358:**

Monday

I am capable of being responsible for myself.

Day **359:**

Tuesday

God has good plans for me.

Day **360:**

Wednesday

I face each challenge with grace.

Day **361:**

Thursday

I can clearly express to others
when I feel hurt.

Day **362:**

Friday

Today I will learn and grow.

Day **363:**

Saturday

I am good and getting better.

Day **364:**

Sunday

Jesus Christ is my friend.

Monday

I can turn every ending
into a wonderful new beginning.

Thank you so much for reading Daily Christian
Affirmations for Teen Girls!

It means the world to us to be able to bring girls just
like you everywhere closer to their faith.

I hope you enjoyed your journey and feel
empowered and blessed.

We'd appreciate it so much if you would consider
going to Amazon and leaving a review.

Your reviews help us bring you more beautiful and
meaningful content like this book.

About Made Easy Press

At Made Easy Press, our goal is to bring you beautifully designed, thoughtful gifts and products.

We strive to make complicated things – easy. Whether it's learning new skills or putting memories into words, our books are led by values of family, creativity, and self-care and we take joy in creating authentic experiences that make people truly happy.

Look out for other books by Made Easy Press here!